A RACE TO THE END

REACHING YOUR HIGHEST POTENTIAL

TERRY LEE MCCLAIN

Gotham Books

30 N Gould St.
Ste. 20820, Sheridan, WY 82801
https://gothambooksinc.com/

Phone: 1 (307) 464-7800

© 2023 *Terry Lee McClain*. All rights reserved.

No part of this book may be reproduced, stored in a retrieval system, or transmitted by any means without the written permission of the author.

Published by Gotham Books (October 24, 2023)

ISBN: 979-8-88775-611-0 (P)
ISBN: 979-8-88775-612-7 (E)

Because of the dynamic nature of the Internet, any web addresses or links contained in this book may have changed since publication and may no longer be valid.

The views expressed in this work are solely those of the author and do not necessarily reflect the views of the publisher, and the publisher hereby disclaims any responsibility for them.

TABLE OF CONTENTS

ACKNOWLEDGEMENTS iv
DEDICATIONS v
CHAPTER 1 Today (February 19, 2016) 1
CHAPTER 2 Just Jump In 6
CHAPTER 3 A Comfort Zone...9
CHAPTER 4 Longevity..13
CHAPTER 5 "Keep moving forward" 15
CHAPTER 6 Stay on Course 18
CHAPTER 7 My Mission 23
CHAPTER 8 The Will to Survive...31
CHAPTER 9 Push Through It..36
CHAPTER 10 Maintaining on the Mountain Top..................39
CHAPTER 11 Pressed for Time...42
CHAPTER 12 Leap for Joy 48
CHAPTER 13 Shine Like a Star 52
CHAPTER 14 Just be You 55
CHAPTER 15 Mind, Body, and Soul..65
CHAPTER 16 Take a Break 70

ACKNOWLEDGEMENTS

I give thanks always to God for the gift of writing. I want to thank everyone (my friends) that has helped me out along the way (in one form or another). Again, thank you all. I want to thank my fiancée Marvelous for her loving interest in my work. My mom, Sally, for her support thus far in my life. My six brothers for being in place when I just want to converse and laugh with someone. And, a very special thanks to my publisher Gotham Books Inc. And Audrey Monroe for giving me the opportunity to display my writing skills to the world. Again, thank you all for becoming a part of my life.

DEDICATIONS

To the many people that need help (Mind, Body, and Soul) around the world. And, to my five grandchildren; Ariah, Duriel "Little Man", Cassidy, London, and Royalty (a new born as of 01/23/2017). Four girls and one boy. I love you all, always.

CHAPTER 1

Today (February 19, 2016)

As long as my knees can bend and my head can bow; I will pray.

Quote by: *Terry Lee McClain*

The United States of America (USA) is to a large degree calm today. I moved around all day today and as I was driving home, I realized that I did not see nor hear of any bizarre occurrences (murder, robbery, rape, etc...) that had drawn my attention. The country was seemingly at rest; like everything was in order. I am a man of many thoughts and sometimes the subtleness of the above settles on my mind. I know that many bizarre events unfold in this country virtually every moment of every day. Yet, I rarely concentrate on the brutal and senseless activities that plague our neighborhoods at the rate of speed as a bullet fired from a gun. I would rather devote my thoughts to all the good that is constantly going on around me. You would just have to lift the dark blinds from your eyes and see the light of goodness shinning all around you. This country is full of milk and honey! The very things people spend their entire lives looking for is actually right under their noses. Happiness and peace of mind is not going to follow you around and beg you to take them. You have to reach out and grab them when the opportunity presents itself. You are the only one that can make yourself happy or sad. Therefore, you have to reach inside yourself to fulfill the desires of your own heart. Hey! There is no one that can fill you up with Joy and happiness like filling up an empty cup. You must fill yourself up with the way you want to feel. No one can do anything for the way you see life except you. My focus here is to allow you to think differently as to how you view the world around you. You don't have to always think and believe the world is falling only on you. Begin to believe in "Something" beyond this world and yourself; then you can perhaps see and feel a change going on inside yourself. You don't have time to continue to always see the bad side of life. Life is passing by like the white lines that separate the lanes on highways and one day you and I will be no more. Therefore, live your life with a positive attitude; free yourself mentally from the general frustrations of life (worry and stress) and all the happiness you ever dreamed of will be yours.

Today, has been a very good one for me. The joy and happiness within me are at a height higher than a giant. To bring you another book forth today is like a basket full of joy and happiness to me. I write to bring you "Hope". My time on earth has been good thus far, because I am still living. I have accomplished much. I define my goals and pursue them. Therefore, I can't complain about anything right now; I am pleased with the position in life that I am in. I always shot to be number one at anything I try to pursue. Again, Today has been a good one.

In the previous two books I have written and this one too. I have named the first chapter "Today". The reason being, I want my readers to know what is going on at the present time in the United States of America. Also, I desire that one day after my life is over; I want people to know how the world and my country (USA) was and my existence in them as an African- American writer. My plans are to see my writings as a monument of history as being told by a man that cherished his existence in a society where very few black people talk about their moments on earth. I want people to know of where I grew up as a child, some history of my family, and the struggles of my past. Also, I want people throughout the world to know that you don't have to be rich or famous in order to be of value to society (I want to leave a legacy for humanity through my writings). I hope to inspire you and others by writing about the experiences of my life thus far (good and bad).

See, I grew up in a time when being poor was common as the common cold for a large number of African- American families (early sixties). As a man now of fifty- two years old; I have witnessed and seen a lot happen in our nation since then (good and bad). I have also endured a lot. I can also say, I grew up in a truly great and wonderful era. I have lived to see many stupendous athletes perform, tremendous actors and actresses in movies and plays, overwhelming musicians, and this country's (USA) first African- American President (Obama). I will always believe that Obama and his vice-president (Biden) have guided this country (USA) back to its feet. I believe the position this country was in during the (Bush) administration was down the scale farther than a lot of people realized. I was looking for our country to be the next third world country under the (Bush) administration. I now see and believe that a major shift in the economy (from horrible to good) has occurred since Obama and Biden took the reins of power seven years ago. I believe our country is number one again throughout the world and I am pleased with that.

The next election for our country (USA) is under way. Obama is almost finished with his eight years in power. I am hoping and praying that it be the will of God to see fit for Mrs. Clinton to become the next president (the first female president in the history of our country). She will do a great job for the people of this country. Trump? I just believe he is not the guy he's portraying. Oh well, let the will of God be done in this particular situation.

Time is really passing by. A few hours ago, I saw one of my grand-babies (Cassidy Connor) turn seven years old. The Birthday party was held at her house in Charlotte NC. Myself and other family members had hot dogs, cake, and ice cream. These are the moments of my life that I cherish the most. To see my family members having a good time. It all seems to put a dark cloud over some of the rough days I have endured in the past. Today, I look back and marvel at how my life once was and how it is now. The transformation and journey have been stupendous. From drinking (Alcohol) excessively, doing drugs, jails, and prisons; to buying a new house, driving a (2004) Ford F- 150, having four darling grand-children, a fiancée, and my freedom. It has taken me fifty-two years to reach this point. I tell you; I could not ask for more of Jesus thus far in my life. And, the best of the above is having my freedom. There is nothing on earth or on a million other planets that I would trade my freedom for. Real freedom cannot be traded for. I would like to tell the young of our society now; having your freedom means almost everything about surviving the rest of your life. See, as long as you are free; the chances to become who you truly can become (Doctor, Lawyer, Scientist, Engineer, etc...) can happen and when your freedom is taken; nothing can happen. I truly believe that having your freedom is the beginning of the path to all the happiness you could ever receive in your life time. A multitude of people have given their lives for this very privilege (many races included). Young people! please, hold on to your freedom. It is not worth losing. You will never gain anything valuable enough (money, respect in the streets, flashy cars, fancy clothes, etc...) to out value your freedom. I could go into countless memories of my own history as a Black American/ African- American man, the history of many black men like Dr. Martin Luther King Jr., and the history of the black man in America. I am choosing here to let you do the research on your own so you can't say I misguided you or tried to twist the truth. Again, cherish your Freedom.

Today, has gone very well for me. I am in no pain and the general frustrations of life are at a far distance from me. I am happy and I will always hope to see many more days like "Today".

CHAPTER 2

Just Jump In

I am writing this book for people that desire more for themselves (better days, better living conditions and a better position in life). The ones that expect more of themselves than they have obtained thus far in their lives. To the ones that want to reach their highest potential as a human being. See, I have obtained many of my desired goals for life; I have reached the pinnacle for self-satisfaction. In this book I hope to give you ideas and ways to reach your highest potential. Again, I just recently bought a new house, drive a Ford F-150, and working on my third book. I want to perhaps show you how to obtain material gain and be happy too. See, it's not the material things that drive me. I demand a high degree of happiness within and I believe that happiness guides me to the material things. Look at it this way, what good to you is a mansion, a Lexus, fine jewelry, a fine woman/man, and fancy clothes if you can't be happy with them? I will always believe that misery loves to have a companion. Therefore, always look for a high degree of comfort within yourself and I promise you all the material things you ever hoped to acquire will come to you. The above is how I have achieved the material things that I have at this point in my own life and I already have claimed the victory that I am not finished. I believe there are many more things to come (a plethora of blessings).

Life is like a hot summer day at the swimming pool. You stand at the edge and can't wait to feel the water; then you jump in without hesitation. Splash! Living your life has to be the same as the scene above. Just jump in. Hesitation causes you to doubt your decisions. You cannot doubt your abilities. You must believe that you possess the abilities to live an almost perfect life. Your life was given to only you. Therefore, live out your life to the best of your ability and train yourself to be happy doing it. If you want a new car, house, or a better position at work; Go get it! It's yours. I believe we were put on earth to prosper; to do good for ourselves as individuals. If it's o.k. for Don across the street to have a Bently; then I feel like it's o.k. for me to have a Jaguar. His may be more expensive than mine; but hey! I got a respectable car too. You must begin to believe that most anything on earth that you want is o.k. to have. Working for what you want to fill your heart's desire is perfectly alright. I have seen a lot of people that hesitate when it comes to living. Again, you can not hesitate. Just jump in and begin to live out your life to its highest potential. Many people could be far more successful if they would stop thinking about what Jennie and Bob next door may think if I get a BMW and concentrate on their next move toward even greater successes. See, I am writing from experience and know you have some of the same type of thoughts as I do (we are all human). Thus, I am sure you know what I am speaking of above. I have been in many situations where the only thing that was holding me back from the success, I know I deserved was ME. I use to think of what others thought of me and it held me back from reaching the highest expectations of myself. Now, I know that by living in America; almost anything can happen. I mean anything! It's like, you can be a vagrant one day and be on Wall Street the next. I am serious, you have the control and abilities to be virtually anything you desire to be in America. Again, just jump in!

CHAPTER 3

A Comfort Zone

The flowers of Spring are beginning to blossom. I have a cluster of flowers in a flower bed in front of our house and three beautiful stalks have opened with a breath-taking orange-reddish color. the blooms open into different majestic colors. I did not know that flowers could produce such mysterious colors. Spring and Summer are my favorite seasons, because they bring out the awesome beauty of nature.

I write in real time and it gives me a great feeling. I want you to know and be able to envision what times are like at this day in time in America. I want you to be able to envision your life as the beauty of the flowers I mentioned above. Therefore, find a comfort zone within yourself and maintain it like a flower bed. I have come to know that it doesn't matter if you're doing good or bad; people are going to talk about you. People will push your name in the dirt just to make themselves appear to be better than you. I am here to tell you; never feed in to other people's negative talk (to you or about you). I use to really bask in the negative talk that others said to me or about me. Inside I would feel miserable and, on the outside, I would appear to be happy. It was as though I was living like the comedian and actor named Robin Williams. He seemed to be so full of joy and happiness in front of audiences and cameras; then killed himself. I learned a lot from that sad tragedy. If you cannot be happy within yourself; there is no way you can appear happy for others and constantly maintain the act. I believe Mr. Williams was never happy inside himself, truly. Hey! I could care less today what someone thinks or says about me. I have fought diligently to accomplish the happiness inside myself I have obtained. I own a feeling that no one can take away and I know my feelings are real. I don't have to appear to people as happy and bathe in misery on the inside. The comfort zone I speak of is a zone of calm you must develop within yourself. A comfort zone that tells you that you truly are happy with being you. A zone that makes you comfortable with yourself. See, many people assume that somebody or the world is responsible for their dispositions in life; that it's the people of the world causing all their problems. I look at it all this way; I make my own calls as to who I am or who I become in this world. It's no one's fault if I decide to run into the street in front of a semi (eighteen-wheeler). A comfort zone is where you deal with who you truly are. Learn to cope with yourself. Many people look for others and materialistic things to guide their inner feelings. when this occurs; they eventually become sad and misguided within themselves. Therefore, you must become happy for yourself and yourself alone; you must come to a point where you know exactly who you are to yourself. Plain and simple, you must become who you truly believe you can be to yourself and other people.

See, a lot of people in my life (fiancée, mother, brothers, and friends) do not know I am writing at this level of confidence. The fact being, because they do not really know the true me. I know when some of them are one day reading my work; they will wonder if it was I that truly wrote of matters as of above. Most of the mentioned people above will not believe that I went to this magnitude to explain who I truly am and who I have truly become as a man. Yea, I have come a great distance to get to the inner feelings mentioned earlier; I did not get to this point over night. I have survived military service, mental institutions (due to military service), three prison sentences (DWI, common law robbery, and crack cocaine possession), alcohol abuse, drug abuse, and a failed marriage. Oh yea, I have been there and done that! And today, I am alcohol and drug free, because I demanded change in my life and inner man. At fifty-two years old, I know I have overcome some difficult challenges. I ran a difficult and awkward course quickly. I have put a lot of unnecessary miles on my body. Yet, I am still here and now enjoying every aspect of my life. My inner man is very happy. The progress I have made in my life thus far is stupendous to me. I know the depths a man/woman can take himself/herself to and I know the heights that can be reached by a man/woman. I have personally lived on both sides (the low and the high). I am pleased with my position in life thus far. I cannot complain.

My overall mission in this book is to get you to the point of happiness inside yourself that I have obtained. I want to ignite a new flame to your candle of self-confidence. I want you to know beyond doubt that you are somebody important to the world and you are just as bright as the stars in Hollywood. My desire is to elevate your confidence to the level of the ocean breaching levies during a powerful hurricane. See, you cannot shine if there seems to be a cloud over you constantly. The key to letting yourself shine as a star is to dismiss whatever negativity that comes toward you or enter your mind. The dark cloud that is covering your happiness is nine times out of ten you or somebody close you (family, friends, or people in general). I tell you; you cannot allow yourself to absorb and soak in the negative mentality of others. Don't let what John said about you to Lucy trouble you. Hey! hearsay can be the number one killer of your happiness. Relationships (girlfriends/wives), family, and friends can destroy your attempts to be happy. Believe me, I am writing to you from a personal view point and realistic experience. Therefore, finding a comfort zone of your own is essential in order for you to seek and find the happiness you deserve. See, you have reached a great point already in your life; you are still alive and reading a fantastic book. Hope is still very much alive in you. I will always believe that the forces that control all existence want us as a human race and as individuals to be happy (and also prosper); to live out our lives with joy and for our hearts the feeling of peace. Think about it this way, why would the creator make a creation that was going to be unsatisfying to Himself? It would make no sense (from my view point). Believe me, you are somebody. Thus, take control of your feelings and love who you are. I believe you are special to creation and anything good that comes your way; you deserve it. Trust me, you can be better to yourself and for yourself. Again, I have been there and done that; at any level you choose. Do as I am doing; set back in your own comfort zone and enjoy the rest of your journey through life.

CHAPTER 4

Longevity

Longevity is a destination in life we all seek to reach. unfortunately, all of us as humans will not reach old age (that's just a true reality). Therefore, be ecstatic for the present moments you live now. don't throw your precious life away. Sure, I would like to live a long life and I know you would too. Unfortunately, we must stare reality in the eyes and accept that some of us as mortals will not grow old. Therefore, I tend not to concentrate on how long I have left to live. I just live. Because, I don't know what is on the other side of life as we know it. I do believe that there is something else after our time is spent here on earth. I often wonder what is on the other side though and one day I will know for sure. Therefore, forever hold your life dear to your heart; because, it is like a wave that rolls to shore, it rolls in with force and a loud sound, then it is gone; forever. I look at most young people today; they think they're going to live forever and some think they know everything about life (that's just my stance on young people at these days in time). They know not those years of experience in life surpasses all the thoughts of a youth beyond measure. I will be fifty-three years old on June 18th, 2016 and I am so happy that I have come thus far. I have made it thus far by "Will Power" (the strength from within to continue moving forward) and the shear "Mercy and Grace of Jesus Christ". To the young I say, if you want to live a long life; take a look at yourself on the inside (identifying the difference from right and wrong) and truly believe in something beyond yourself. Believe me, it took years for me to get to this point to where I can attempt to guide someone else in the right direction. I created many troubles for myself in the past (Jail stays and prison stays).

I am here to tell you and anybody else; you do not have to travel a rugged path as I have taken in the past to become comfortable with who you are and what you really want to do with your life. Trust me, I had to look at myself deeply inside and decide truthfully as to what I wanted for the rest of my life. I decided that jails, prisons, and the street life was never going to allow me to be the person I always knew I could be. I have come to the point in my life today that I can say, if I die right now, I am happy with where my life came from to where it is now. I am alright with me. My hope is that your life will to extend far beyond expectation and you reach old age. I just want you to know that I ever hope the best for you and your life. I straightened my crooked path through life and I know you can do the same. Longevity is a precious goal to reach and your life should be cherished like a priceless piece of art.

CHAPTER 5

"Keep moving forward"

The time to decide your fate for your life is "RIGHT NOW". You have control of your own destiny. Yea, we all know that there are forces that created us and earth. Unfortunately, none us knows exactly how long we will live. And, by now you should know that (whatever you choose to believe in) cannot do everything for you. Some things about life you have to decide for yourself (that's just reality). Therefore, the stage is set for you; you can decide to keep moving forward or continue to go backwards for your life's sake. I have decided that I would keep moving forward with my life. If you keep waiting on your life to change directions on its own; you will be waiting like waiting on a bullet to return to the gun from which it was fired. I decided that I was the only one that could make the best decisions for the direction I wanted my life to go in. You must do the same. Go ahead! take yourself on a new journey. Stop believing that your life is worthless.

Once I decided deep in my soul that there are some things in this world you just cannot do in order to maintain a free-living life style. for instance; stealing, robbing people or businesses, shooting guns at innocent people, drinking alcohol excessively, and doing drugs. Believe me, you will go to jail, prison, or the grave yard eventually. Therefore, I basically live a life free of any mind controlling substances and take each day as it comes; one day at a time. Thus, take some time to yourself and "TRULY" decide the direction you want your life to go in; forward or backward.

Today, July 10th, 2016. I am still morning within for the death of my aunt, Margaret "Duck" Ross-Starns. She passed on July 5th, 2016 from bone cancer. She was a great person. She worked hard and took good care of her family. I truly loved her. I didn't attend the funeral services due to unforeseen circumstances. As one of my favorite aunts I am writing about her that her name will continue on. She may not be remembered by many years down the road, but I will always remember her for the rest of my life. She was taken so suddenly. She didn't get to grow too old; although, she left behind a son; Bryant Starns, two grandchildren, and a loving husband (Ricky Starns). Like I say, some of us will never see longevity in life. Therefore, go for the best for yourself right now; you don't necessarily have to live a long life in order to make a good impression for yourself that others may live by. I write these things because, I love my ancestors; the living and the dead. I want you and others to know some of the history of my family. I have looked at it this way, if longevity is for me; good. If not, Amen. I intend to make the best of the rest of my life no matter how or when it ends. I am going to live like I know my aunt "Duck" did; live it fully until it ends.

CHAPTER 6

Stay on Course

I am fifty-three years old now. I have had a lot of dark periods in my life of the past. Periods when it seemed as though I could not go on another day. Today, I live a completely different life style. The life I live now I am proud of. There is not much I wish to change about it. If someone would have told me seven years ago that I would have a nice house, truck, and a fiancée today; I would have never believed them. I would have told him/her that you are completely insane. See, I left old habits behind me. I changed my course. And I say to you today, I stay on course. I had to make some critical decisions for my life in order to maintain my sanity and freedom. I say and I am telling you these things because I want you to improve on your way of living. I write to give you the experiences of different hardships that I have overcome in order to give you the chance to choose a better direction for yourself. The methods I use to stay on course is: I had to respect myself first, put away drinking (alcohol), doing drugs, step away from "street friends", abhor criminal activity, and keep the faith in Jesus Christ. I speak of Christ, because he has been the best Icon for me to follow (believe in whom you choose). I love the gospel. Time is based on His Holy name. Therefore, in order to maintain a free and respectable life; you must reorganize yourself as I have above (do what works for you). Again, do what works for you. Trust me, everything else surrounding your life will work itself out. I do want to remind you that I do not live a perfect life; I don't live on a mountain top glazed over with doughnut icing. Thus, you should know by now that virtually everybody has "something" they're attached to (good and bad). Everybody has different habits of some form. I say it this way, there is a little something going on with us all. I do have difficult days and I have my ways also. Yet, most part of every day I feel happy and free inside. And, I am thankful! So, if leading a better life for yourself is a vision of yours; then I strongly suggest you look "seriously" at what is going on with you now and develop the determination to carry out better days for your life. The determination is within you. It has always been there. You are the same person now that you were as a small child. You just have to see things different from here (RIGHT NOW). Now is the perfect time to readjust your life and move forward with it. I believe we (as humans) was created to be model figures for all creation and to present ourselves to each other with love and respect. We were put on earth to be good examples for humanity and to live with respect toward the creator. I truly believe that there is something "HOLY" about all creation; that there is "Something" out there far beyond earth that spiritually put all creation into place. You can call it whatever you may.

All I know thus far is that we come into the world and stay for a while and then we leave. Therefore, keep believing (in something) and let it be what guides you through life and keep you on course. Life is like a large ship at sea; it must stay on course in order to reach its destination. Thus, you cannot reach your goals or become successful unless you stay on course. I will give you an example from my own experience. Thirty-five years ago, I was perhaps one of the most powerful young black teenagers in the USA. I went to work in a cotton mill at age sixteen in 1980; attended a two-year college (Gaston), had my own apartment, plenty money, the finest of new clothes, credit of superior shape, nice car (1976 Monte Carlo), good friends. With all the above I come to eventually realize that I didn't know what I had; I had the world in the palm of my hands and didn't know it. See, growing up I was never really introduced to the business sector of life; we (my brothers and I) was not taught how to invest or plan for the future. We made plenty of money picking strawberries for the Linebarger's at that time (middle seventies to early eighties) and didn't know what to do with it. Now, going back to what I was saying above about being on top of the world as a young man and not knowing what I had. I eventually walked off from the cotton mill job due to a misunderstanding with the plant manager. Then, I began to steer off course. I tried to pursue the Mechanical Engineering field I was studying in college and was unsuccessful (due to "some" prejudice people) at that time (1980's). I eventually joined the Navy and I continued to steer off course from there. I just recently (within the last five years) got back on course. Therefore, I tell you from true experiences; you cannot detour from what you have set in your mind to do for your life. Again, 'You' must stay on course in order to reach your destination.

See, when you and I was growing up we wanted to be something- I believe it's in most of us from the beginning of life. We wanted to be Nurses, Doctors, Lawyers, Engineers, etc... Then, as adults the drive (motivation) becomes blurry. We steer off course (Alcohol, drugs, and the street life). Some steer back on course and some don't. See, I believe the primary problem with the homeless man, drug addict, alcoholic, criminals, and prostitutes are that they just steered off course from what their aspirations was growing up. They are not all bad people (something the justice system should really consider in certain cases). A majority of the time when people are put in jail or prison it's not really because they're bad people; it's because they have steered off course from what they previously wanted out of life. And (sadly), many never find their way back on course. Mainly, people get caught up into a cycle and don't know how to get out. The way out is to dig deep within your soul and seriously decide what you want out of your life. Then, choose a good path to follow and begin to redirect your life. See, I have always figured that no one else can change a person but that person. I had to change me. No one else could bring me to the reality I needed to see. I saw the true reality and pleasure of living as soon as I walked out of prison (Hopefully for the last time) in 2011. I have not looked back. Hey! it's all in the mind. The way you think decides your destiny; PERIOD. Therefore, in order for your ship to remain on course; you and only YOU have the power in your mind to guide it into port. It doesn't matter how bad your life is or was; you can begin to change right now. I just believe that people get caught in a cycle- as I spoke of earlier. They get into running the streets (drinking alcohol excessively, consuming drugs, and hanging with the wrong type of people, etc...) to the point that it becomes o.k. to live that way. They become comfortable with the street life. I have learned from pure experience that the cycle can be broken. Just think of it this way, when troubles surround you like a gang of cowboys; don't surrender, just look up to the heavens and call on the Lord Jesus, and let Him fight your battle. Then, everything around you will work itself out for the good. I have also looked at it this way; everything you have been through (good and bad) was a test of your strength, determination, and will power to get you to right now. If you are reading this book as of now; you still have a chance to change the direction of your life. Because, if you are reading this book; you are still alive and I truly believe that you still have the chance to become anything you want to become (Doctor, Lawyer, Engineer, Minister, etc...). I can't say it enough, if you want to lead a better life, the time is 'Right Now' to decide what you want for yourself for the remainder of your life. Hey! get on course and stay on course.

CHAPTER 7

My Mission

The primary thing that keeps me going is my mission. My mission is to leave a legacy for you, my nephew AJ, my four grand-children and perhaps the world. I want to know that you are alright where you are right now. That you have read and understood my writings. I want someone to grow from reading of my life experiences. The ultimate signature on my life is that some people have changed their lives due to my writings. I have said before, I wish not for richness; I just want to be comfortable (financially) and love my neighbor as I do myself. I have four grand-children (London, Cassidy, "Little" Duriel, and Ariah) that are my inspiration for leading a better life than I once did. At this point in my life, I have come to the understanding that it is not about me anymore; it is about the little ones. They must go on! Our country (USA) is in need of great people like my grandkids as they are today- So precious. Therefore, through my writings I hope to continue to guide them, you, and others in the direction of leading a rewarding life style.

The road to my present state (at peace with my life) has not been easy. And I wish not that your travel through life be more difficult than mine. I wish great things for you and others. My primary objective for writing is to let you and others know that life can be pleasant to live if you are willing and determined to want better for yourself. Period. I use to not care if I woke up for the day or not. I was once so deep in despair and discomfort about my life that I felt as though my soul dwelled in a cave. The main problem for me was alcohol abuse and too many encounters with the law. To the young I tell you, the law is like a spider web; you get caught in it and you may or may not get out of it. It can become a cycle as I have spoken of earlier. Today, I stay away from anything that could possibly produce an encounter with the law (drugs, alcohol consumption, criminal activity and domestic violence, etc...). And don't get me wrong, I have nothing against the police; nothing. For I feel this way about it all, think of what the world would be like without policemen. Right now, in this country (USA) there has been a rash of police shootings of seemingly innocent men (mostly black men). I look at it this way, policemen are human; there are good ones and bad ones. And sadly, the bad ones are sticking out and waving like the checkered flag at a NASCAR race. It is just another trend that will have to cease on its own (like the school shootings and the drive-by shootings that plagued California in the 1990's). See, trends are often like a smoldering fire; sometimes you just have to let it smother itself out.

My hope is to bring you to a reality that many will

never accept. that your life and the lives of others is controlled by unseen forces (good forces and bad forces). See, I believe that all of it (good and bad forces) has to be present in order for society to function. Like the animals in the jungle, the good and bad have to collide in order for the ECO system to function. If you look at it close enough; humanity works the same way. I say it like this, it's not all about just ME and YOU. Nevertheless, it's alright to lead a happy and prosperous life. Think on this, has anyone told you lately that you couldn't have a nice family, nice car, nice house, etc...? Hey! I tell you, there is nothing wrong with leading an upstanding life. You just got to accept that the ways of the whole world are not going to conform to just you and what you want the world to be like. The world as a whole doesn't care about how your life ends. Although, I have a firm belief that the last state of a man/woman is his/her best testimony. I want my end to be glorious like an actress gleaming in beauty on the red carpet. You have to decide for YOURSELF as to how you want to carry out the days you have left to live. I tell you; I live life today on the natural (no alcohol use and no illegal drug use) and I feel great about living like this. It is an everyday walk with belief leading the way. It's called leading a normal life-if there is such a thing. I get up in the morning excited as to how the day will proceed and how it ends. Therefore, my mission is to leave you with the true impression that I decided for myself to lead a good life. That I gave my very best to society. And, that at some point in your life you will be satisfied with the progress you have made.

There is a lot of things going on in this country (USA) right now. The latest trend is bad race relations between black people and policemen (as I spoke of earlier) and race issues throughout this country. I am not racist in any form or fashion toward any race. I am puzzled as to why some people in this country think they are better than other races; that this country is theirs. My question to such people is? What makes you think that you're better than others? Is your blood a different color than red? what gives you the right to believe that you were made different than other people? Yes, I am black and I am never going to change that and I am thankful that no one else can change it either. I look at it this way, can a Pelican change his instinct to dive for fish? can the golfer change the flight of the ball once it leaves the club head? And, can a Zebra change his stripes to spots? Therefore, I cannot change the color of my skin like an actor/actress change costumes during a play. I was born this way and if you dislike me because I am black, I feel sorry for you. See, the sky diver can't change his parachute once he/her have jumped from the plane; neither can a man/woman change the color of their skin.

This country has been plagued with this color non-since for centuries and even at this day (August 27,2016) and point in time; some people have not changed and sadly they never will. Like I have said, I write in real time that you may know also of some of the harsh realities going on at this point in history in the United States (USA). It is just a regenerating cycle of hatred; like in the earlier parts of the twenty-first century up until now. I say it like this, Dr. Martin Luther King Jr made a major impact on the world with his life and he was determined to seek justice for mankind (not for just black people) but for all men/women. Thus, I can say it like this; I have likened my life to that of a race (marathon). There is a start and an end. So, whether you're black, white, tan, or mixed; we're all in a race to the end. You came into this world to start the race and you shall leave this world to end the race. What do you want for your life in the time frame mentioned above? What will you have done with such a beautiful life? I just want to break the tape victoriously; whether I am first or last. Think about it, where are we (society) really going? See, all of this (existence) was created by something or someone far beyond human imagination and we as human beings was created for a special purpose. I believe that we were made to represent the Creator in order for Him to demonstrate the power of His goodness. I truly believe that existence was formed by something scared and very Holy. You can think what you will and I will think what I will. Look around you close enough and you will see for yourself that my words have a good base for truth.

I have always competed against others (brothers, cousins, and neighbors) as I was growing up. My six brothers and I have competed against each other since we were small boys. We could play basically any type of game. My brothers and I have always wanted something to win at. We played cards, shot marbles, played monopoly, horse shoes, football, basketball, hop scotch, fishing, swimming, and foot races. We wanted to compete and win at nearly any cost. We all eventually became athletes during our elementary and high school days. I became skilled at wrestling and was quite good at it. I had a combined record of fifty-six wins and five loses from the sixth grade to the eleventh grade. Two of my brothers (Timmy and Anthony) became star high school quarter-backs. Timmy was also skilled at wrestling. He was runner up in the North Carolina State Championship two consecutive seasons. Therefore, the stage has always been set for me to compete. It is in my blood and I love it. I now look at living life this way: The runners are at the starting line for the twenty-six-mile marathon. The race official holds the start gun skyward. A single shot is fired with a deafening sound. The runners are off and running. The stadium explodes in to sounds of cheers. One will win and one will lose. The others will place somewhere in between. Their placement is decided by their own determination and their abilities given by God. I believe that some things were just meant to turn out the way they do; that sometimes there is nothing we can do to determine the outcome of an event or situation. For the winner, the race will be rewarding (a victory) and for the loser, the race will be disappointing. Therefore, the question here is? Where do you want to place in this race of life? Do you want to cross the line victorious or cross it in defeat? I just want to cross the line; knowing I finished the race. Even if I am last and get into heaven; I will still feel victorious. The moral here is thus, we are all in a race to the end. My hope for you is that you want to cross the line as I do; to finish the race. Nevertheless, "I am in to win".

I believe we was put on earth for a purpose and given the chance to decide the impression we leave for God on the lives of our loved ones and others. To be a positive impact on humanity. My mission and purpose (I believe) are to depart this world having left an everlasting impact on someone's life. That I did my very best to give you a good understanding and example of what God purposed for mankind. That I did my very best to help you lead a better life style than you may previously have lived or is now living. I truly believe we all have a purpose for our existence and that we decide the destiny of our purpose. I will always believe we was put here (on earth) for the battle between good and evil spirits; as spoken about in the scriptures of the Bible (King James Version).

The battle between spirits beyond earth and the human perception. The ultimate sacrifice for humanity and all existence being fulfilled at the birth and death of "The Great Counselor" over two-thousand years ago. Therefore, you don't have to be first in a race to the end; you just have to be determined to finish; as Jesus did. You get one chance to live, as I believe. Therefore, do your very best at life and get the most of everything your heart desires (materialistic). It is o.k. to own things as long as you never lose sight of God. Always, put God first and everything else you desire will come to you. Again, life is like the sky diver speeding toward the earth; he cannot return to the plane. Therefore, when you leave this world; you cannot return.

It is Saturday September 10, 2016 and I feel as though I have reached the pinnacle of my life. I feel as though God has blessed me immensely at this point in my life. I could not ask for more at this junction. And as I have said, my mission is to bless you through my writings; that you will begin to navigate your life in a new and exciting direction- as I have. You need not to look back. I believe your future will unfold into prosperity like the shine of glitter! Again, my mission is to give you hope for a better future. And when my days be over on the earth, my ultimate achievement and satisfaction is that I brought to you my very best work; that from here and the rest of your life you will become successful (lead a better life). Again, I have reached the pinnacle of my life and success; mentally, spiritually, and professionally. I feel as though I cannot reach higher for anything else. I have searched the depths and heights of my inner man. I have come to my final conclusion about life. No one can lead a good life if distracted by the bad experiences of his/her past. Therefore, my advice is that you leave your past doings behind and concentrate on moving forward. I tell you this, everything that you have gone through in the past has prepared you for "Right Now". And look at it this way, if you are reading this book, you have made it through whatever you have gone through. Everything you have gone through was to bring you to "Right Now". See, I believe that more than half of the reason that you may or may not be where you want to be is because you are still stuck on what has happened in your past. Believe me, your past is gone like some relatives that have visited you and left; waving as they leave. You can't get your past back. I feel that it's o.k. to reflect back on memories and sometimes the mind just takes you back. I am saying, in either case; you don't have to linger there or dwell there. thus, you must move on; like a cowboy leaving at day break.

Ultimately, I hope to give back to society. To let you and others know that "I Tried" to give you the best experiences of how my life once was and now is. I feel if I can demonstrate through my writings how to lead a better life, if my work changes one person on this earth; then my mission will be accomplished. I must mention this, I didn't get this far alone. I have had good friends to help me along and I wish to say, thank you all for anything you have done for me. Nevertheless, I know beyond any doubt that God has kept me under the shadows of His wings.

CHAPTER 8

The Will to Survive

The will to survive, I will use myself as an example. I grew up in this country (USA) in the 1960's and 1970's. During those times we basically lived as a poor class family. I was not born into a wealthy environment. I was born into a family that had a loving mother and daddy though. We lived mostly around the Kings Mountain NC area; an area West of Gastonia NC called Ebenezer. Ebenezer was essentially a black neighborhood occupied by cotton mill workers, farmers, and hunters (Rabbits and Squirrels). As children (my brothers and neighborhood friends) we were taught at an early age how to work hard to earn money. We picked strawberries, hauled hay, picked plums, and gathered pecans to sell. We also played cards for money (often unknowingly to our parents). My brothers and I was skilled at competing. We played games often; nearly every game that was known of at that time. We played anything from Jack-Stones, pitching coins, and pitching horse shoes. We tried almost anything that would give us a chance to win or make a dollar. Therefore, the will to survive was embedded in us (my brothers and I) from the beginning. The instinct to survive is still very much alive in us today. We have always strived to be better than the next person (competing); at anything and on any level. Today, all seven of us continue to strive to be the best at what we pursue. The will to survive instinct is still realistic in our lives today. My brother Timmy has his own law firm in Orlando FL (USA) and I am a Navy Veteran with an honorable discharge (GO Seabee's!). Also, my brother Rogers landed a job with the Coca-Cola company that has sent him to school for four years to train in maintenance. My other brothers also, have manufacturing positions that pay very well. Thus, we all have respectable life styles. I have said the above to say to you, you must develop the will to survive instinct in order to maintain a decent life style. Period. I mean, there is not too many other ways to accomplish what you seek for your life. I know because I am a living witness that the above is true. You can make it to anywhere you put your mind to make it to. You want to be President, do it. You want to be a Doctor, Engineer, Lawyer, or a Scientist; "Do it". There is nothing holding you back but you. Nine times out of ten we tend to shoot ourselves in the foot "per say". We tend to create our own problems.

See, life is about surviving; how long can you endure life from day to day? Longevity is reached on the bases of how you have survived. You have to go out into the world and make something happen. A good life is not going to come and grab you by the arm and say, come on.

You have to go out there (into the world) and get it for yourself. You have to be determined to live beyond your own expectations. I have done just that; leading a life today that I never expected of myself five years ago. I tell you, me and my brothers have come a long way thus far. We all are still living. The youngest is thirty-eight years old. Therefore, during the hard times as children we learned how to survive. I eat, sleep, and breath the will to survive. It was instilled in us by our daddy (Robbie, RIP) of whom died in 1999. My daddy did it all, from growing gardens to killing hogs for many different people (he really knew how to make a dollar). He set an example in me that he never knew of; bend but never break and never stop dreaming. I have followed that example to this very day. I am satisfied with how my life has turned out thus far. Again, If I die right now, I have lived a good life.

I went to work in a cotton mill at age sixteen in 1980. I was hungry for success from the beginning. I was very established by the age of twenty. I had anything a young man could want. I was diligently determined to win at life. I know today that even then I was in a race to the end. That success and the materialistic things I desired would not come to me easily. I somehow knew then and I do know now that I am in a race to the end. I have to run this race to the very finish. See, in a race to the end; a multitude of things will occur (good and bad). It's all like a marathon race (our lives); you must run twenty-six miles in order to finish. Again, a multitude of things will happen. You may stumble and fall, drop your water, or just quit from fatigue. And you may win! Nevertheless, it's up to you and you alone to determine how you want to finish (first, last, or somewhere in between). I will always want to be first or near the top finishers. All I know is I don't want to end up in last place; except, it be the last spot left to get into heaven. I will gladly take that spot. This is how I view life and existence. A race to the end. The race can be filled with excitement (owning a house, having a family, drive nice cars, etc...) or defeat (homelessness, alcohol and drug use in excess, divorce, jail, etc...). It's as though we are all competing for one thing or another. Thus, I look at life like this; you are either winning or losing; or somewhere in between. Again, it will always be up to you as to where you want to finish. Ultimately, a race to the end is about where you want your soul to rest when this life is over. For me, I would have it as you and I crossing the finish line together! That when this life is over, we will have accomplished more than we could ever have imagined. That our lives were a success. Yea! as I have mentioned before, it is my mission to get you to a victory. I want to be your coach. Through my writings and experiences in this book; I want you to eventually be at the top. As I have said, I believe I am at the pinnacle of my life. It would satisfy me the most to see you happy and established as I am today. Believe me, you can be where you desire to go with your life. No matter where you are right now (divorce, alcohol and drug abuse, homeless, unemployed, etc...); you possess the power to redirect your life. You must first define within yourself; your meaning of a will to survive. A good reason to carry on with your life from where it is now. which is what this chapter is primarily about. I tell you; I have been through the highs and lows of life. Therefore, the decision is yours; what will your life be like at the end? what will you have accomplished between birth and death? What will be your legacy? And what are you doing right now to improve your life style?

See, I never got comfortable with the street life.

Somewhere in the forefront of my thinking I would say, to myself; I know I am better than this. I eventually lifted myself up and made my way to a better situation; to where I am today. Basically, I had the will to survive. It didn't all happen overnight. It has taken years to get to where I am now. There were many falls along the way and the odds of me succeeding was near zero. Today, I know that it was determination and the will to survive that kept me going. Therefore, my questions for you are; How do you want your life to go from here (forward or backward)? What will you do for yourself in order to survive? My hope is that you will absorb the meaning of my writings to you and put what you have been exposed to into action. Believe me, it works! The key to unlock the door to your happiness is will power; the very will it takes to win a race. How will you proceed from here in order to survive? what will you do next? I say to you, get up if you have fallen and go your way; You can make it from here with the will to survive! Ultimately, how long do you want to live? And what sacrifices will you make in order to survive? The ball is in your hands now; will you shoot for the game winner or will you pass up the chance?

CHAPTER 9

Push Through It

The time has come for you to accept reality. Life is not always going to be like the glaze on a doughnut. You are at a point where it is critical that you make some life changing decisions. Go ahead, look around yourself right now and see if I am lying. See, I know your situation right now; because I have been there. I am speaking mostly to you and people that are not doing well at this junction in their life. Again, I speak and write from experiences that I have endured. I speak to the people that may not have their life going in the direction they desire. I mean, what they truly desire for themselves and their life in the deeper chambers of their hearts. See, I know that if things are not well with you right now; your desire is to be in a better situation. Again, I have been through nearly all of the highs and lows of life. I lie not. I have been on top (materialistically) and on the bottom (homeless).

Nevertheless, in the deep recesses of my mind, heart, and soul I desired better for myself. Never during the times, I ran the streets did I ever accept that my life would remain as such. I just never accepted that it was alright to live that way. Therefore, a major problem with you and others is the fact that you have somewhere in your mind, heart, and soul accepted your present state. Sadly, you have become comfortable with the way you are living. Your self-esteem is near zero and the feeling of not caring about what happens to you the very next moment has consumed you. You feel as though you have nothing to look forward to and nothing to live for.

I tell you, there is hope for your present state and it is inside of you. I used that hope one day and used it to do something with my life. I had to diligently search within myself to summon that hope. I was at the point I spoke of above. Today, I have looked back on many bad situations I found myself in and I discovered that life is similar to an obstacle course. You will run into many obstacles along your journey of life. Period. Ultimately, you will have to conquer the obstacles or fail the course. You will have to go over the obstacles to get to where you want to go. You have to climb over them, go around them, or go through them. See, everything you have been through (good and bad) has brought you to right now. Hey! if you have made it thus far; you can go farther. And, in order to continue on with your life you have got to "Push through It". You have to push through whatever comes before you (relationship problems, alcohol and drug abuse, thoughts of suicide, unemployment, and homelessness, etc...). I can proudly say, that I have truly pushed my way to a decent life style by pushing through obstacles like the Juggernaut bursting through a concrete wall. I tell you; you have got to push through it; no matter what comes your way. I have done it this way, I first developed confidence within myself (that I could do better with my life) and I have never given up on the grace and mercy of God. I know for sure that He has had mercy on me. Ultimately, I never gave up on myself nor my dreams from youth. I always dreamed of doing good for my life. And today, I believe my faith in God, Jesus Christ, and The Holy Ghost has made my dreams come true. believe me or not; if you never lay down your faith you can overcome anything. And I mean anything! My question to you is? Do you believe in yourself enough to "Push through It"?

CHAPTER 10

Maintaining on the Mountain Top

The most difficult task is not the climb to the mountain top; it's maintaining on the mountain top once you get there. In other words, keeping your life organized once you have reached the pinnacle thereof. Meaning, your work is never done; it is only beginning.

I have also likened my life to that of a mountain climber. The mountain was very steep when I got there and the terrain was very rugged. The higher I climbed the more the terrain became difficult to surpass. I got tired often and wanted to turn back, because the obstacles became more and more challenging. It was as though I just could not surmount another obstacle. I even had to stop off in a cave; just to rest and to somehow summon my mind to carry on. The cave was dark and cold. After resting a while, I made my way back to the climb. I finally reached the summit. I was elated and raised both arms toward the sky in victory. The climb to the top was over and I was ecstatic. It's like once you reach the top and look back at the challenges and obstacles you faced along the way; It is as though none of the danger and challenges I faced even mattered. The victory has been accomplished. That is all that matters to me. A great feeling!

Now, the real task is at hand. How do I maintain on the mountain top? What do I do with my life now that I have reached the pinnacle thereof? See, I described the event above to give you an example of how life really is. Again, It's like a climb to the top of a mountain. You will encounter many things that will try to stop you. Therefore, you must never give up on the task you're trying to accomplish (reaching the top); becoming successful. And, once you accomplish your mission you must continue to maintain your life as though you were living your last few days on earth. Maintaining on the mountain top becomes critical and you must continue to organize your life. It is as though the game has gone to over time. Once you believe you have reached the top, don't just stop and sit down on yourself; always keep it moving. At this point in your life, you have a great chance to make up for the mistakes of the past. Now, you have a chance through my writings to make things right with yourself. No, I am not God and will never claim to be; I just know certain things from my experiences through life thus far that you may not know. Therefore, my overall mission in this book and two other books I have written is to give you a short cut through life without having to take the rigorous path I took. The path I took I wish for no one. To the young people I say, today times are different for you than they were for me. You don't have work too hard (cotton mills, construction, and general labor) to make a living in order to survive; you have the opportunity to use your mind (through education) to make all the money you will ever need. Trust me now, the doors of opportunity are swinging open for you today like the doors of a saloon during the cowboy days of the old West. Thus, I am telling you, take advantage of the opportunities that come your way and do not be afraid to create your own opportunities. Always find a way to keep yourself going; within the legal realms of the law. Maintaining on the mountain will be the most difficult part of your journey through life; I lie not. And don't let jealousy and inappropriate friends pull you down (back down the mountain). Therefore, take what you have learned from my writings to you and use them to the best of your abilities. I wish you well on the rest of your journey through life.

CHAPTER 11

Pressed for Time

The most valuable gift given to existence was "TIME". I say this because, time has been my friend through thick and thin. Time will give you all the chances in the world to get things right in your life. You have a chance to start your life over anew right now. See, we are all pressed for time. You and I did not come into this world to stay. Our time is not long on earth; we all as a humanity will pass away one day. Time will go on, but we will be transformed to another type of existence. Therefore, use the time you have now very wisely and take out a little time from your perhaps busy day to give thanks for your situation (if life is good for you). You can thank whomever "You" choose (God, a bike, or a six-foot-tall chip monk). I prefer God, Jesus Christ, and the Holy Ghost. Because, that's the spiritual realm I believe that is in me. I have no problem with what you may or may not believe in; it is not up to me to decide your ultimate fate.

We often do not like to talk about our ultimate fate (which shall be death), although it is a subject of fact. I start and end my days with this fact in my heart and soul; I am happy to be comfortable with knowing that one day I will be no more in the earth. At age fifty-three, I know I am ready at any given time to meet my creator. Thus, begin to learn to accept your ultimate fate; you will be a lot happier in this life. I know, because my life has taken a stupendous turn in the last several years and I am very pleased with myself. I am happy that I have been given the time to redirect my life. I speak to you as such, stop wasting your time rushing to gain materialistic things (which is o.k. to have). Nevertheless, and moreover, put time into yourself and your soul. Materialistic things will come to you out of the blue sky (per say). Material things don't last always, but your soul will continue on after this life (at least that is what I believe). I am not in the vocation of preaching; I believe I was put on earth to merely teach. Teach people how to lead better lives. I am speaking to you in a positive sense, because I wish better things for you.

I am pressed for time like a bird building a nest. The bird is always working fast as though its next breath will be its last. Therefore, spend the rest of your time on earth making things better for yourself. I tell you; no one will ever care for your situation if you don't care for yourself. No one will care for you better than you can care for yourself. See, I once lived in despair and had no care in the world as to how the next day would turn out. I was just at a point where I did not care what happened to me. Then, one day the light came on inside my head. I had to decide if I wanted a better life or spend the rest of my life behind bars or in institutions. Believe what I am saying, my life came to the very point above. Today, I know I made the right decision and I am very thankful that I did. Today, I own a nice pick-up truck, three bed room house (in Gastonia NC), and a fifth grand-child due by February of 2017. My fiancée' and I are getting married in 2017 also. I am not telling you these great things to appear to be bragging. I tell you these things, because I desire that great things will happen in your life as well. Again, we are all pressed for time. Therefore, try to get things in order with yourself first; and I promise you the materialistic things will come to you.

      I have worked many years of my life (physical hard labor). Now, I set back and take life easy. See, I did like the bird; I built my status fast. I worked as much as I could and as fast as I could during the early days of my life. I basically retired at age forty-nine (became disabled from military service). I have done my very best to succeed and I truly believe I have. Above, is just a small part of great things that I have accomplished in my life thus far. My greatest desire is that my soul is ready to return to my creator when my life ends on earth. Therefore, do not take the rest of your life for granted, because it can end in the blink of an eye. Cherish your life, because it means something. You are not here on earth by accident; you're here for a purpose and it's up to you to find that purpose. Trust what I say, if you believe in yourself great enough; you can make manifest virtually anything the mind can conceive. You can change your status right now in order to lead a better life. As I have said, I have been down on the bottom of society and I know what it takes to reach the top. I am mostly speaking to people that are on the low side of life and desire to lead a life better than the one their living now. Nevertheless, I speak to all people of all races, because whether you are doing good for yourself or not you still may need guidance (make adjustments or improvements) for one thing or another in your life.

I do believe (from experience) that there are thousands of people in this country (USA) that want to lead a better life and the only thing preventing them from doing so is the fact that they have become comfortable with their present life style. They have accepted their present state. I tell you nevertheless, redress your mental attitude and refuse to accept your present state (no matter what your state may be right now) and believe in yourself strong enough; You can become virtually anything you put your mind and heart into (Doctor, Lawyer, Nurse, Carpenter, etc...). You can also have the life style you truly want for yourself (nice cloths, a house, cars and trucks). Hey! there is nearly nothing you can not accomplish. See, believe me or not, we are all here on earth on borrowed time. Let's face it, you and I are going to be on earth just for a little while. Since I have been living, I have not seen a change in the course of how we come into this world (birth), stay a while, and leave (death). I have not known of nor saw anyone return either. It's fact, reality, and truth. Therefore, as I am doing at this point of my life, I desire that you would come into more understanding of the realities I have spoken of above. Hey! Face it, at some point you have to accept reality for the truth that it presents. I am understanding more and more each day about just plain ole "Reality". Again, I am where I am today, because one day many years ago I refused to continue living as I was. " YOU " can get where you desire to be in life also. I know you can and most of all I believe you can. And, once you reach the top; never forget the people that helped you along the way. Again, never forget; because you might see the same people coming down. For, no matter how long you stay on top; you must eventually come down. The old saying goes, what goes up must come down is truly a statement of pure truth (trust me and believe me). I thank everyone that has been a part of who I am today.

I often think of how my life could have turned out thus far. I tell you, there is no measure of payment I could give to my maker that would thank "Him" enough for what He has done for me.

Yes, my time is limited here on earth and I plan to use every breath I have left to live to present to you the very best way of how to lead a better life. Again, we are pressed for time. You can begin now to reorganize your life; you have all the time in the world! See, the mystery of life is; we know not how long we will live. Therefore, would it not be better that you have lived well now and going forward than to have suffered twenty or thirty more years? Whatever is hindering you from leading the life style you truly want to live (relationships, alcohol, drugs, domestic abuse, etc...); put it behind you and move forward with your own life. See, something or someone gave YOU a life to live. If you feel that you cannot do these things alone; Do Not be too proud to ask for help. Missions, AA, NA, churches, and local government agencies are standing by with open arms to welcome you. Trust me now, the only way to receive help is to ask for it (the worst outcome is they say, "NO") and the word NO will not kill you; just ask someone else. I told one of my brothers (Roydell) one day, that if people tell me NO a thousand times a day it does not matter; the only thing I am looking for is the one YES. Pride will destroy you and I tell you right now if you are spending time at intersections and curbs; you don't want help. You will never pull your life together by standing at a curb hoping somebody gives you some change. Hey! If you are in the circumstance above and have made it thus far into this book; "GO" get some real help. If you want better for yourself, Go get some help; help is out there...

CHAPTER 12

Leap for Joy

The true feeling of happiness in my heart is awesome to me. I look at the beauty around me and it makes me want to leap for joy. I have come to understand the beautiful structure of the word "Reality". Reality to me means, standing straight up as a man/woman and accepting the responsibility for all of my actions. Therefore, if your life is not in the order to represent reality; then step back and truly glance at your past. your past actions are a reflection of the life style you live right now, "Except"; you have made different adjustments to your way of living (good changes). I tell you; you will "NEVER" live out a decent life (law abiding and outstanding) without making positive adjustments along the way. You must conform to reality (as mentioned above) in order to lead a positive life style.

I will give you a great example of how making adjustments daily can make a major difference in your path through life. A few weeks ago, me and my momma was in Asheville NC to visit my uncle Woodrow Ross (my mom's brother) at the V.A. (Veterans Administration) hospital. He is in a fight with cancer. He was in great spirits though and is now doing "O.K.". Me and my mom left the hospital after an hour or so. We also visited my brother Roydell (Roy) of whom have lived in Asheville NC for over twenty-five years. Roy celebrated twenty-five years clean and sober this past September 23rd, 2016. (My feelings of Joy for him for his accomplishment and the love I hold within for him are just overwhelming). Me and momma got relaxed a little after we arrived. Roy and his family of four (his daughter "Punkin" was out with some friends) was elated to see us; they were happy beyond words. His son "Kendrick" was ecstatic and of whom this section of the book is the example spoken about above. Roy's wife "Karen" was happy to see us as well. The example involved Kendrick as I said. The conversation among us all was scattered (everybody talking at the same time) and Kendrick was telling me about his grades in school (6th grade). He was telling me that he wanted to bring up his "C " grades to "A's" and "B's". I told him, that he could; that he was above average. I said, there is nothing wrong with being average ("C's"); that a "C" was not that bad. We talked about it only a few minutes and finally, he said, Uncle Terry I am going to bring those grades up to A's and B's. I truly believed him too. That was as I said, a few weeks ago. I was on the phone with Roy yesterday when Kendrick came home from school. As me and Roy was talking Kendrick said, Daddy; I made A's and B's on my report card. Roy was happy and I was just ecstatic. Sure enough, He had pulled his grades up to A's and B's.

The moral of the example given above was to let you know that making the adjustments necessary to become better at what you desire for yourself is possible. The adjustments can be made in an instant, if the desire to change comes over you strong enough. Desire and determination will crush low self- esteem every time if you have the will power within to fight adversity. You have to battle with adversity in order to achieve success; it is just a part of life. You and I are not immune to this universal fact. You are dealt a hand(cards) and you must play what was dealt to you; no exceptions. Therefore, play the hand you have been dealt to the best of your ability. Give yourself a chance. Hey! often I look at the pair of deuces (2,2) I feel as though I was dealt at the beginning (growing up). I look at my hand now and I see a full-house (Two 2's and three A's) and I love it. So, Yea! I have come back from a long way down in order to reach the top. I refuse to look back now. I am maintaining on the mountain top and the future for me looks to be even more rewarding.

I was on the porch moments ago and it all hit me like a left hook from "Frazier". Hey! this is the "Promise Land" (USA). I stood a moment and breathed it all in. I am free! I tell you, I wanted to leap for joy. Here I am standing on our (my fiancée and I) front porch gazing at the stars. It is like this, I am free to go virtually anywhere I want to go if I just suddenly wanted to go somewhere, I live in the USA, and I am able to do what I love to do (write) without nearly any restrictions. This (USA) is truly got to be one of " The Lands of milk and honey" as spoken of in the scriptures. I am amazed at the number of great things going on right now in this country. Again, it is truly a joy to have lived in an era such as I have (1963 to present). There have been so many great things to happen I can't begin to tell all. I do count president Obama's rise and reign as the number one event that has occurred during my life time thus far. I cannot think of a more staggering event to have come to fruition in this country during my race to the end. I mean, as a young man growing up I "Never" imagined America would eventually have a Black American/African-American president. It blew me away and I am ecstatic that it happened.

    I have spoken above to let you know that you too can leap for joy. Leap for joy for the changes that are going to come into your life henceforth. Hey! be thankful that you are breathing right now. Life is beautiful and should be given thanks to. I tell you, it's only three days before Thanksgiving and I am truly ecstatic. I am super ecstatic, because I am truly thankful for everything that is going on surrounding my life right now (good and the not so good). I am just telling the truth. Life is not always going to be peaches and cream. I couldn't be more thankful! If you work at life hard enough, God will send you blessings. Sometimes, you just have to set back and soak in happiness like a woman soaking during a bubble bath.

CHAPTER 13

Shine Like a Star

I have given you the best of the best of me and my life experiences. Therefore, believe me when I say, I care about your wellbeing. I care about your circumstance and situation as it is right now. I write to those whom want to better themselves and their life styles. See, I am a living witness to a truth that I now live; almost anything can happen in America for your wellbeing if you choose to change your way of living. The impossible can materialize (houses, cars, and good times) if you have the desire in your heart to never give up.

The one thing that keeps me going is I have developed an understanding that nothing is going to come to you freely; you have to go out into the world and get whatever it is that you desire to have. I know how to shine like a star, because I have believed in my heart that there is no one on earth any better or worse than myself. I truly believe that at this point in my life I have become an everlasting star to the world. I have given back through my writings and I often give back with my heart. I write to let you know that I would desire that you would change your life in order that you can shine like a star as I do. I tell you, in this race to the end you have one shot to make the best of your life. Stop beating yourself down if you're not where you think you should be. Just begin now to give yourself a fair chance at leading a good life. See, I have been through the rough times. I can sympathize with you and your current situation. Again, give yourself a chance. Today, I am proud of myself and overwhelmed at the changes I have made in my own life. The road that leads to misery I have traveled, I finally decided to take a turn and now I am on the road to prosperity. You have to look at life this way, I am here (living on earth) and I may as well do my very best at it. And you can. Believe me, you do not have all the time in the world. Even a long life is short. Therefore, get the very best out of yourself while you still have some time left. Hey! If I can change and make a difference in multiple lives, so can you. The time is now for you to make the greatest decision of your entire life. Do I remain as I am or do I want better for myself? Your answer will follow you all the days of your life left here on earth. My guidance and advice throughout this book have been for you and you alone. Take heed that you do not forget the spoken words above. They are the words that will decide your fate from this moment forth. I brought these truths to you sweet and bitter, because I had to accept the very words spoken above myself one day. Hey! This is not a game of pool we are playing here; this is your life and the remainder thereof that is being spoken of throughout this book. My reason for writing these things is to get you to believe (in yourself). I have realized that the only way to make a difference in the lives of other people is to look in the mirror and change yourself first; then you can make other people feel comfortable with themselves. Hey! Life is all about who you are as a person (kind or sinister) and what do you want to be remembered for (YOUR LEGECY). Basically, what did you do during your life time to contribute to the wellbeing of society? Therefore, look at it for what it is worth; take the light that is within you and shine it around like a flash light. Don't let darkness be your guide. Shine like a star, it is O.K. to shine. To shine like a star doesn't mean that you are bragging or being boastful. Hey! Let the light in you glow while it's still shinning. For, the light in us shall not shine on earth forever. Thus, begin to see yourself and your life style shine like a star; then watch yourself sparkle like a new diamond ring. Believe me, it can happen; you can shine like a star. You just got to believe in the very light that shines in you.

CHAPTER 14

Just be You

The time has come in your life to accept reality. The reality that the world cannot change who you are or who you become. It is time to paint the real picture of your life. See, numerous people all over the world paint a pretty picture of their lives each and every day. They live a fictitious life and paint a pretty picture for the public. Millions of people live like the above. I will give you an example. Again, there was an actor named Williams that was a comedian/actor and he was very talented. He was funny to millions upon millions of people around the world. He seemingly lived the perfect life. He presented himself to the world as one of the happiest human beings to ever live. And low, this same guy hung himself. I think the tragic incident happened in 2016. It was near the top of the list of the most tragic deaths to happen since I have been living. I was sad beyond words. I was like, not this guy; he was one of the happiest of people I have ever known of. See, with this man I had an untrained eye as to the life he was really living. I would have never ever thought the man was sad and depressed most moments of his life. Again, it truly was a sad and tragic death.

above was described for a very special reason. That reason is why I write. To get you to understand that there are real problems in this world that real people face. I write to try putting you in a frame of mind that the very life within you is real. That your daily existence is not like a wrapper on a candy bar that you just through away. The examples I give throughout my books are meaningful (never forget that). Too, my writings are to make you a better human being. I perhaps will never come to you to put you down; I will always try to pick you up (for, I know where I come from and how far I have come in my own life thus far). I came in this world for a purpose and I believe my purpose here is to help other people; to be that guide to steer people in the right direction. Therefore, if you are painting a pretty picture for your life; please, stop. Period. Just be you. See, you also came in to this world for a purpose (and I believe you came for a good purpose). The Bible (King James Version) says, the poor will always be among you as spoken by Jesus. I believe I don't have to be one of the poor. My thoughts are just like that. Although, I am aware of the fact that I can become poor at any moment; I just keep my mental attitude on a level beyond the negative things that can happen in my life. Therefore, you too have a choice as to how you want to carry out your life. You don't have to paint a pretty picture of your life before the public. Again, just be you.

See, during my days of high school (1979-1981) I was a person that analyzed other people and I remember how so many people in my classes acted out the fit- in-part. Just wanting to fit into the crowd. I didn't have a slew of friends like most of my class mates. I just wanted to be myself. I really wanted to just be me and the humble person I wanted to represent. I look back on those days and I am happy that I didn't change just to be part of the crowd. And, even today I believe that not much has changed about myself. I am an easy-going person toward people in general and I harbor hate in my heart for no one. I don't flip and flop my attitude from day to day either. If you meet me today, I can say, I will be the same person you meet tomorrow (nine out of ten times). I tell you; you cannot be yourself and be like somebody else at the same time. You will either accept yourself or choose to try being like someone else. Trust me, to choose to be like somebody else is very dangerous. Again, just be you. And I promise you that at the end of the day you will feel better. If you begin to feel as I do about life, you can truly find happiness and that is to feel that everything about life "Is what it is"; no more no less. I tell you; you will only get out of your life what you put in it. I promise you that. Therefore, begin to think on this level. If I don't choose the right way for myself and my life; who is going to? Hey! I have been there and done that as the saying goes; many times. I am now a living testimony for you and others that perhaps you will not follow a path such as I did in the early days of my life. My point here and throughout all my books thus far (Three) is to allow you to shorten the distance between failure and success. I am only trying to guide you on a different path than I took. Therefore, the remainder of my own successes will depend on the successes you create for yourself. Again, my primary objective for writing is that your journey through life be not as difficult as mine. Believe what I am telling you, I know and am very aware of the fact that other people have had lives far more difficult than my own. I am not saying that I am the only one on earth that have had a rough life. I just want you to know that your life does not have to be difficult nor complex in order to fulfill the desires of your heart. Thus, I will sum things up this way, forever and ever follow your dreams; if you believe you can make your dreams, come true then give it a shot. Follow any of your dreams and if you truly believe that you can make them come to fruition; they will come to fruition. Never let anyone shoot down your dreams and I mean anyone. Just be you and you can become the next anything (pilot, engineer, carpenter, president, or electrician) the world can use. There is a saying on the side of the recycle trucks that come through my neighborhood here in Gastonia, NC that says, "Go Green" as for the environment. I say to you, for your life and the remainder thereof; "Go Positive" as for the wellbeing of your future and the lives of your loved ones.

I enjoy who I am today, I would not want to be anyone else. I said the above, because I truly am who I am; me. It is a Plato rarely reached. To be you and only you and be happy therewith. I give the military nearly all of the credit for giving me the mental training to overcome most anything the world throws at me and I mean anything. I feel like I would not be living today without the training. I am just being real. See, I don't write for the fun of it. I write from the experiences I have lived through. All I am saying is, get the most out of your life while you still have it. Again, this is not a game we are playing. Life is a serious matter and I take my work at writing very serious. So, take what you read of my work and use it to the best of your ability. Remember, we are in a race to the end; it is just that simple. I plan to cross the finish line. I would have it that I might break the tape and run on into heaven. I tell you; I am trying to be one of the best finishers of all time. In my heart I am running now, reaching out for the tape. I just believe that when it's all said and done for me and my life; I will be a top finisher. Therefore, if you feel as though you're running this race a little behind time. Look up and keep running, the end is not as far away as you may think (your break in life is just around the corner). Always, keep your head up and belief in your heart; and you will finish this race also (in a good fashion). So, gather yourself right now and press on. I want you to run in front of me or at least alongside me. Again, my writings are to give you confidence and determination that no matter your position right now in life; you can overcome your situation. I know what is like feeling as though you are on the bottom of the earth. I am telling you; I have been in nearly every bad situation the human mind can summon. And I know a man or woman just cannot lie down and give up. I just believe that it is just something in us as humans that will not allow us to give up (completely). And think of it this way, if you lie down on yourself; then in whom would you trust to help you up? Therefore, you must begin to stand on your own, because there are just some things the forces refuse to do for you. Thus, if you are in an alley, on a park bench, at a shelter, alone, in an abandon building or under a bridge; I understand. Although, you don't have to live out your life in your current situation. If you have read thus far into this book, then you should know at this point that you can make it. You can live again. You just have to get up now and go forward. Forever leaving the past behind. I believe you can have a major impact on the lives of other people like I am trying to do. You must begin now though. See, in our race to the end there is no more time left for complete foolishness. Excessive drinking (alcohol), illegal drugs, running the streets and so on and so on. The time is now to put away those foolish types of behavior. You must get serious about your life and get down to business with proceeding forward with the remainder thereof. Depending upon your age, the time for the race to end might not be too far off. Again, I am just being realistic. Remember, most of or nearly all of my writings are from my own experiences. So, I am not joking or just writing to put useless words together. In all honesty, I write to give you hope. The kind of hope I had to grab and hold onto for dear life. The hope of living a better tomorrow. I tell you, the worst feeling I have ever experienced during my life thus far, is the feeling of lying down hoping tomorrow never comes. I have had only a few nights of this nature, and I don't want to repeat any of them. If you have not experienced this type of feeling you are doing better than you think you are right now. It is the worst feeling I have ever experienced during my life thus far. I would wish this feeling on no one. So, right now I can understand your circumstance and still I will tell you that you can be O.K. again. The words I am writing are real and they are written to help you back to your feet. Therefore, help me help you up to your feet and we can finish this race to the end together.

The new year 2017 is here and day one has been wonderful. It has rained most of the day and for me that is alright. The 1st day of 2017 came in calm; it came in like a well-trained pilot lands a plane without flaws. I've said once before that I love writing when it is raining and that remains so. Today is Sunday and my feelings are comfortable. I and my future wife went to services today at the church we belong to. The service went smoothly as usual with no outside interference. My heart and soul will always go out to the nine African- American people murdered during one of their weekly gatherings by a young European man in Charleston SC. This type of cowardness is the reason I always pray for myself and you (because your life can end in an instant). Moreover, I know God gave everyone the choice in whom we should trust; Him or to do evil. The young man that took the nine souls from earth will receive his reward in the end. I can say no more. I just hope the new year brings peace to more hearts. Overall, the day has been stupendous. My fiancée and I ended the day by going to the movies to see the new movie called Fences. The acting was fabulous by all the actors and actresses involved. After the movie we returned home and relaxed a while then fell off to sleep. Again, the first day of year 2017 was a blast for me and I am hoping and praying that the rest of the year goes well.

      I wrote of the above to give you a clear idea of how life is for me at this point. I say to you, you can live a life also that gives comfort to your heart and soul. Hey! You just got to remove yourself from your present situation (no matter the circumstance) and begin to repossess the thoughts you once possessed of having different dreams and aspirations. Take the opportunity I am speaking of and lean on it; I guarantee you not to fall. Also, begin to understand that the world was not created for just you. You have to learn how to accept the reality of existence as it truly is. Accepting the good and the bad that enters your life from day to day. Again, I can relate to your current situation. I like too, the saying by a lot of people that say, you don't know my situation if you have never been there or you can't tell me about alcoholism if you have never consumed alcohol. Believe you me, I have overcome a large number of situations and circumstances that seemingly had no solution. Just be you and things will turn around for you. Again, I write to give you the best of the best experiences of my life that you may achieve great things in your own life. I tell you; the remainder of your life does not have to be lived out as you are now. The greatest opportunity to lead a better life is unfolding right now before you. By reading of my experiences thus far, you can begin now and in a short time span you can accomplish great milestones that still exist for you. I say from here, if you desire to have a nice-looking house; go out and get it. If you desire to have a nice-looking car; go out and get it. I am just saying, you can have the desires of your heart (materialistic things) at any given time; you just have to want them bad enough. Believe me, this is your world too; begin to get out of it what you believe you deserve. Again, just be you. This book was written to give you the best opportunity perhaps in your life time to reach your highest potential. You were born with the perfect instincts to achieve maximum success. Take the chance now to redirect your life while it's available to you. I will never steer you in the wrong direction. My primary aim is to get you out of darkness and into the light. The kind of light that cannot be dimmed. The kind of light that makes you glow like a candle in the midst of total darkness. See, I believe we (you and I) was put on earth to glow like a light upon a light house in dense fog. We were given a soul and it was never meant to be covered by darkness. Therefore, Let the glorious light in you shine. Just be you. Hey! It is alright to shine like a new coin. You just have to have this type of belief within yourself. And, you can feel this way about yourself without anyone knowing it. It's Okay to be happy inside. I know too that every day is not as pleasant as a walk in the park. See, life is virtually composed of having good days and bad days. Good feelings one moment and bad feelings the next moment. I know of this type of days and moments, because I have lived through them. Again, I am not a perfect human being. I do have flaws of my own. I just continue to work on myself continuously and keep moving through life with a positive attitude. I have learned to be satisfied in whatever state I am in. Whether it be good or bad. I am comfortable with who I am today and that is all that matters to me. Through it all, I am just going to continue to be me.

The focus of this chapter is to allow you to take a minute and reflect on yourself and your past life. And, asking yourself; Is this where I want to be in six months or even five years? The basic question being, what do you want for the remainder of your life? Happiness or misery? These are some of the questions I had to answer in the past. I had to get real with myself and get serious about my life. I was at a point once that the situation was either live a life of freedom among society or spend nearly the rest of my life in durance. I feel today as though I made the right decision and one of the best decisions I ever made. Therefore, I know that a person can change; because I did. I believe too, that anybody can change. Period. The solution to nearly all of your problems (no matter what you are faced with) is within you and how you approach circumstances mentally. It is the drive of the true desires of your heart that will sustain you through the rough times and the good times. See, I know you did not just wake up and decided to be homeless, use alcohol excessively, abuse drugs, or stand on the corner asking for change. I know that once before in your life you desired to be something (Doctor, Gymnast, Football player, Nurse, Airplane pilot, etc...). I tell you; you can still fulfill your aspirations and dreams (perhaps in a different form from what you intended initially). If you cannot play basketball any more due to your age or physical abilities; do not let that stop you from becoming an Electrician or Engineer. Hey! No matter your age, it is never too late to return to school or get professional training for what you may desire to be. Again, just be you. Go back in your past and search for that little boy or little girl that wanted to be that Nurse or Tennis player and bring that person forth. You are still that person. All I am saying is, give yourself a chance again. You deserve it. Give yourself a second chance. You did not come to earth to fail. I just do not believe the creators of existence created us (the human race) with the intentions that we all should fail.

CHAPTER 15

Mind, Body, and Soul

The time will come when you have to put everybody and everything going on in your life to the side; then concentrate on yourself and yourself alone. If you want to lead a better life; then you have got to put some work into it. You have to dive into your life with Mind, body, and Soul.

Everyone has a story to tell. Although, most people choose not to tell his/her story. Therefore, I have no problem telling my story. I truly believe that my story can help people; even you. I decided some years ago to put order back into my life. I had to dive into my life like a platform diver at the Olympics. I had to utilize everything within me (mentally) to pull myself back together. At one point in my life (early thirty's) my self-esteem was so low that I could hardly hold my head up. I was drinking alcohol excessively, doing different drugs (crack cocaine included), running the streets like a wild animal, and living homeless. I was going back and forth to jail and prison. I was in a mess and I knew it. Nevertheless, I continued to believe that I would not live as such always. See, I never took my mind off my dream of leading a better life. I tell you; I have been where you may be right now. Believe me, I can sympathize with you in your current situation. I know the feelings of being alone in this world with no one to talk to. These are the reasons that I write to you. I eventually came to the conclusion that I did not want to live out the rest of my life is such a manner. I used my Mind, Body, and Soul to free myself from the misery of immoral behavior. Here again, I know what it is like waking up in the morning with nothing but the next breath you take. Having no money, no cigarettes, no coffee, and no friends. You feel empty inside. You look back at the night before and realize that just a few hours ago you had six-hundred dollars in your pocket that you worked an entire week for. Again, I know what it is like to live immorally. And, I could go on and on. My point being, I can basically relate to any and all situations and circumstances you may be faced with now. Again, I released myself from that type of nonsense with my Mind, Body, and Soul. I used my mind to relate to myself (that I was all that mattered), I used my body to free myself from the street life; I just refused to deal with it anymore and I used my soul to free myself from the misery that goes along with living the street life. I had to believe in something beyond myself and I decided to believe in the Christian deity. I tell you, when you wake up and realize that you are wasting your life away; then and only then will you seek help or begin to help yourself. See, I believe and will always believe that it has got to be the individual himself/herself that wants better for himself or herself.

No one else can make these types of decisions for you. You can go to countless A.A. (Alcoholics Anonymous) and N.A. (Narcotics Anonymous) meetings (my hat is off to any and all members). If you yourself is not ready to change your life style; then it is never going to change. Again, only you can decide what you want for yourself. Therefore, use your Mind, Body, and Soul to find out what is best for yourself and your future will glow like glow-in-the-dark material.

The time and the season to move forward is now. See, I know that you have a purpose for society. There is a reason for your existence. To you I say with sincerity, find your purpose. Do not waste your precious time caught up in the cycle of the street life. I believe you too are a better person than you have displayed in the past or even right now at the present. Remember, all it really takes to overcome just about anything is to utilize your Mind, Body, and Soul. With these three resources you can conquer nearly anything. I tell you, learn to understand that this world we live in was not created by itself. There is "Something" (call it what you may) out there far beyond our human imagination that put creation into motion. I mean no disrespect toward any other religions. I Just believe in the elements and forces that I have been exposed to. Therefore, you have a soul; utilize your soul to reignite good feelings in your heart. I will say it this way, the public eye can only see what the individual heart expresses. Express the best of yourself and the world will see the best in you. I am just saying, there is a spiritual justification for all of creation. Some things cannot be denied. I truly believe that the center of all creation is spiritual. I mean, I did not build a cow, give flowers blooms, make water falls or give a mountain its height. Hey! Let's be real for once. Also, "Something" gave you and I a soul that is a living manifestation of some type of creator. Respect the spirit within you and your future will be brighter. Trust me, I did not just wake up this morning and became fifty- three years old. I have tested the waters (per say). I have been to the heights and depths of life. I know the inbounds and out of bounds. And this is why I write to you. I do not want you to have to travel down the rugged road I have traveled. I want you to have a good life early. Leave the street life, work hard for what you want (a real job), believe in "Something" beside yourself, change friends, and always keep hope in your heart; then your life will take off like a jet from an aircraft carrier toward prosperity. Again, we are in a race to the end. I am still running and I hope you will soon pull up alongside me; then we can finish this race together. My prayers are that you and I live a long life (a marathon). Therefore, keep your head up always and keep running. Continue to put one foot in front of the other and you shall reach your destination (the finish line). And when our lives are thus finished and we break the finish line tape. I want to stand with you in heaven and pump both fists above our heads as an expression of victory. And all the host of heaven sing out, "Good Race My Friends, Good Race"!

It is my hope that you have enjoyed this book thus far. I will continue to pray for you, myself, and all others. I hope also, that you have benefited in one way or another from reading this book. I just want you to know that I care for you and your well-being. I know there are many people in trouble right now (in one form or another) and need help (someone to talk to) or someone that will just listen to you. I write for the very purpose above. Again, my primary reason for writing is to give people like yourself HOPE, HOPE for a better future. So, get to running; you got a race to win!

CHAPTER 16

Take a Break

The way to recover your life is to take a break. Take some time out of your daily schedule (whatever you do) to focus on yourself. There is no one more important in your life right now than you. I tell you, you have to stop sometimes and let everything going on around you cease. Give yourself time to think through your next moves (for your life). Life is similar to the game of chess. Every move you make must count or you will lose. You and I are no exceptions to this. Life for me is grand right now and I am grateful for it. Even so, I still have adjustments to make in my own life. I do not know everything. I do know how to conduct myself among society at this point in my life. Therefore, worry less about your past and look forward into your future. You have time if you decide now to get a grip on where your life is going. Again, take a break. The world is not just going to suddenly disappear. It seems like in society today everybody wants everything "Right Now". Let me tell you, my life did not change overnight. It took time. I had to slow down and think about me; just me. I found that life can catch you like a bug in a spider web. You can become stuck in your present situation (comfortable with the way things are now). Also, you can become so overwhelmed with rushing to do this and rushing to do that; then you forget about yourself. You become comfortable with the world as it is. I had to take time out to figure out who I really was and what it was I wanted out of my life. I found out that I am a gem that needed polished. I needed to be reformed like clay on a potter's wheel. I never gave up.

I hope you have enjoyed my work and apply the advice herein to your own life. I have done my best to pave a new road for you to travel. I believe you will do well moving forward. I have very much enjoyed writing this book. Therefore, pace yourself and keep running. I hope to see you cross the finish line with me in this race to the end. I was once lost and did not know where to turn or in whom to turn to. I somehow found a way to get my life back and you can too. I wish the best for you and the remainder of your life. I hope that from reading this book you will go forward and do great things with your life. Hey! Take your time and focus on just yourself. I believe you have plenty of time left to redirect your life and become a positive member of society. And, know too a reality to life; it will not last forever. Thus, clear your mind and continue on from here. I know and believe that you can be the next success story. Period. Perhaps a good family and a stupendous life style awaits you. Go get it. It is all yours. Trust me. See, the great thing about America is opportunity always has its arms open to anyone that has the courage to step out into deeper water. You can be on top today and on the bottom tomorrow. You can be on the bottom today and on top tomorrow. It is just that way in America. Anything can seemingly happen; I mean anything. To have nice materialistic things (money, cars, houses, trucks, etc...) is always obtainable. If you work hard for what you obtain; you can have virtually anything. Therefore, stop believing that great things cannot happen for you. I tell you, It can. Also, you have to breath "Determination". It is the key that unlocks the door to all the treasures of this world. I am living proof that determination, courage, and a made-up mind (doing for yourself what has to be done) will change your life. I will say this time and time again, good things await the determined mind and bold heart. I never began to move in a positive direction with my life until I made it clear to myself that a change for me had to come. I got out of the quick-sand of misery (running the streets) and sought help through the Veterans Administration in Salisbury NC. The obsession for me was to get help. To you I say, if the V.A. (Veterans Administration) is not an option for you; then seek local help (churches, shelters, community organizations, etc...) or state help (Social Security Administration). Help is available anywhere and at all times. No one really has an excuse at this day and time. Thus, go for it (whatever you may seek). Go get it!

It has been truly a pleasure to come to you. I hope with all my heart that you will benefit from reading this book. Again, Go for it! Time is running out (it is reality) and reality will never change for anyone. Thus, muster the strength to keep running your own race to the end. Again, give yourself a chance. As long as you keep running; you are still in the race.

I am starting to pick up the pace in this race. I believe I am in a good position at this point in my life (at fifty-three). I am in to win! I cannot see the finish tape yet and I hope I run this race a long time (have longevity). Even so, I am going to keep running until the end. I say to you, enjoy your life (find happiness) and obtain the desires of your heart (a family, house, car, truck, boat, etc...). And never lay down your faith; never. Always believe in "Something" (even if you want to worship a bag of popcorn). It is all up to you as to what you believe in. Nevertheless, go after your desires with your whole heart and never look back; you will be fine. Yea, we are all in "A Race to the End".

Trump did become our (USA) 45th president. All I can say is, let the will of God be done for this country and everyone therein. Amen!

Author, Terry Lee McClain

Continue to pray for me as I do for you and all others.

THE END.

www.ingramcontent.com/pod-product-compliance
Lightning Source LLC
LaVergne TN
LVHW041544070526
838199LV00046B/1822